THE BRIDGE AND THE BEND

A SELECTION OF POEMS BY
MAHMOOD MUSTAFA

© Mahmood Mustafa, 2019

Publisher: Cheryl Antao-Xavier

Copy editing: Saleem Syed Ali

Creative Direction: Anwar Mustafa

Cover Image: Unsplash.com

Published by:
In Our Words Inc.
inourwords.ca
inourwords2008@gmail.com

ISBN 978-1-989403-09-9 (paperback)

All Rights Reserved.
This book may not be reproduced in whole or in part, stored in a retrieval system or transmitted by any other means, electronic, mechanical, photocopying or other, without prior written permission from the author, except by a reviewer, who may quote brief passages in a review. For permission, please contact author at: m_nmustafa@hotmail.com

ACKNOWLEDGEMENTS

....

Just beyond *'Crossroads'* stood the *'Bridge,'* and, a little further, the *'Bend'*, so it was only natural for me to lead my readers to these next two important milestones in my long and fascinating poetic journey.

Since publishing Crossroads And Beyond in 2015, I have been blessed with a tremendous outburst of poetry. Of course, it was not possible to include all of it in this new collection. I have, therefore, selected 56 poems written over the last four years, along with four shorter poems from my 1982 collection, Beyond the Horizon.

I would like to thank everyone who supported me, and lovingly helped put The Bridge And The Bend together. The project would not have been possible without my publishers, In Our Words Inc., placing their trust and faith in my work for a second time. Of course, the major credit for this goes to the Publishing Mentor, Cheryl Antao-Xavier, whose professional yet friendly approach in helping put a book together is commendable.

Like always, my very special thanks to Professor Dr. Aqueil Ahmad for his sincere and excellent foreword. Dr. Ahmad has now written forewords for three of my books, and I will forever cherish his contributions. My very special thanks to the renowned international scholar, Professor Dr. Munir El-Kassem, for again so carefully and painstakingly going over a very sensitive and important portion in this selection, and making valuable suggestions.

The editing of the entire manuscript was done by my dear friend and thorough professional, Saleem Syed-Ali, a senior copy editor at the Tampa Bay Times in Florida. His meticulous editing and sharp insight are much appreciated.

And finally, my very deep and sincere thanks to my son Anwar Mustafa for yet again producing an outstandingly handsome cover and for his creative input in the design of this book.

Last but not least, my very special thanks to my entire family for their support and encouragement over the five decades in this journey of the verse!

My sincere wish is for my readers to read, understand and ponder over these poems. You may find some of them to be the translations of your own emotions and thoughts, for life often throws up similar experiences and circumstances on our different individual paths.

In life, I have mostly tried following William Blake's advice: "To see a world in a grain of sand and a heaven in a wild flower, Hold infinity in the palm of your hand and eternity in an hour ..."

Mahmood Mustafa

CONTENTS

Dedication	1
The Supplication	3
The Glorious Morning Light	4
The Days That Are No More	6
And When Do I Remember?	7
Beyond 150 And Beautiful	9
A Long Way To Go	11
One Day, Someday	13
The Mystic Sage	14
Call From The Past	18
Couchiching Revisited	20
Mevlana, Salaam	22
Those Sufi Days	24
Drive To Squamish (BC)	25
And All At Once	27
The Awakening	29
The Bridge And The Bend	30
The Golden Chronicles	31
Footprints In The Sky	33
To My Good Friend 'B'	34
The Journey Continues	35
And How Many Will You Deny?	36
In Memoriam	38
Homewards?	40
Hope And Fear	41
Ibadah	43
Elveda Turkey!	44
Lone Audience	49
Perpetuity	50
Iqbal's Message	52
Patterns	53
It Is .... Now!	54

Wind In The Wilderness	56
A New Journey	58
Luqman, To The Progeny	59
Perceptions	61
Remember Me	63
Kavanah	64
Remembrance	66
Sans Winter	67
The Beloved Of All	68
Bay Of Fundy	69
The Break-Up	72
The Distance Is Short	73
The Irresistible	74
And The River Flows On	76
Affranto!	77
Once Born	78
The Other Side	79
An Evening Of Calm	80
Take Courage!	82
Those Hidden Fangs	83
To Have Loved And Lost!	84
Colours	86
The Falls	88
Jihad	90
The Divine Mandate	92
But If The While....	93
Cheap Trade-Off	94
A Dirge To Newtown	95
Your Abode	97
About The Poet	99

FOREWORD

By Dr. Aqueil Ahmad

....

It looks like my friend Mahmood Mustafa, the poet, is at it again. I am honoured to have been asked to write a foreword for this anthology of poems, like on the previous three occasions.

This anthology too, by and large, follows his usual free verse form. It displays the poet's passions, commitments, and concerns for the human condition on the local and global scales. It has been inspired by both Western and Nonwestern philosopher-poets like Rumi, Tennyson, Iqbal, Shakespeare and others.

I remember an Indian poet long ago suggesting that a poet aspires to provide a spiritual link between God and human beings, between the natural and the supernatural in myriad ways. I am not sure whether it is intentional or implied, but I do see spread through Mahmood's work a dose of spirituality that would be appealing to a whole lot of his readers. It shows right there at the start with the Prophet asking the Almighty:

> "O my Lord!
> Expand me my breast;
> Ease my task for me;
> And remove the impediment from my speech,
> So they may understand what I say."

Next, the focus shifts to the beautiful mysteries of the natural world displayed through the changing of seasons when the summer turns into spring, the breeze gets cooler, flowers bloom and a "riot breaks out in the garden – with sweet smelling flowers gently blowing around." And the cycle repeats itself. And lo and behold, it is now autumn. Fruits ripen. Leaves are turning colour. As Einstein would say, "God does not play dice" in the clockwork precision of nature. It is the abundant beauties and countless mysteries of nature – like the Bay of Fundy lying between Nova Scotia and New Brunswick — that seem to inspire Mahmood's poetry a great deal. Could this be the bounty of some divine, blessed feet? Of course, seems to say the poet!

And a lot more! His is a positive message of courage, forbearance, and hope for the best, for life's journey has never been a bed of roses. Struggle is what makes it worthwhile. The cowards cave in. The braves move on. They reflect, resist and rebel against cruelty and injustice. That is how the world is livable, and worth living in.

I had noticed in Mahmood's past work a longing for the life he had left behind but enormous love and respect for his adopted country – Canada. It is once again reflected in this anthology as well. Originally a journalist, Mahmood served for nearly quarter of a century of his career in the immigration and settlement sector, including 11 years as a Settlement Services Manager helping immigrants and refugees in Canada find meaningful work and a new life. This experience seems to have given him a unique sense of an immigrant's role and responsibilities in a great country like Canada. His poetry may have some special meanings for that growing cohort of people across the world, as well as for anyone else with a cross-cultural background.

Mahmood continues to muse on subjects of cultural, historical and social nature, emphasizing their importance and value in our present age and world. He focuses on legendary and celebrated personalities and monuments, and at times, on momentous events, drawing lessons both for himself and his readers. As in his earlier works, Mahmood does not forget to remember, with some joy and some sadness, old ties, old friends and old haunts, reflecting on meetings and partings that mattered.

And so, we have *The Bridge And The Bend*!

Dr. Aqueil Ahmad is currently a freelance scholar in North Carolina, USA. He has MSc and PhD degrees in psychology from Aligarh University in India; graduate studies in sociology at the University of Pittsburgh; and a senior postdoc NIMH fellowship at Northwestern University. He has held sociology and management professorships at the University of North Dakota; Administrative Staff College of India, the University of North Carolina–Greensboro; Elon College; and Walden University. He was a visiting professor at Lund University and a visiting scholar at the East-West Center, the British Council, among others. He has published 7 books, and contributed extensively to academic journals and papers. He has travelled across Asia, Africa and Latin America lecturing on S&T policy and international development.

DEDICATED TO

....

THE BELOVED

"Faithless is he that says farewell
when the road darkens"

....

J.R.R. TOLKIEN

THE SUPPLICATION

And so prayed the Prophet*:
"O my Lord!
Expand me my breast;
Ease my task for me;
And remove the impediment from my speech,
So they may understand what I say"

And I do beseech:
"Grant me the ability and the courage
To speak the Truth
With clarity and conviction,
With simplicity and honesty
And above all
To love all beings ...
Big and small!"

---

*Prophet Moses (Peace be upon him)

Mahmood Mustafa

THE GLORIOUS MORNING LIGHT

Beloved …
By that glorious morning light
When the sun gains height
And spreads its magnificence,
Yet pales off
In contrast to that unmatched glow
In your beautiful face;
By the stillness of the night
When it spreads and covers up …
Very much like your dark, scented tresses,
That cascade down your charming face
Partially covering it and
Making it more exquisite and radiant,
How can you be forsaken?
Or be displeased with?

You are the Beloved …
From time immemorial,
From the time you were chosen,
And indeed the Future …
Each coming era, each emerging phase,
Each arriving moment …
Will be better and superior
For you than the one that has departed,
Bringing greater
Distinction and renown,
And you will be
Blessed and bestowed with such abundance
That you will be well pleased;

For you, there is dignified shelter,
And through you
There is refuge for the destitute,

For you, there is care
There is guidance,
For you, there is independence,
So Beloved, treat not the foundling
With harshness, nor repulse
The supplicant unheard,
And highly acclaim and declare
The bounties at your disposal.

Mahmood Mustafa

THE DAYS THAT ARE NO MORE*

"The days that are no more" are the days that will live
In our hearts and our minds and continue to give
A few tears, some joy and that sweet aching pain
To remember, to hope and long, till we meet again!

The days that are no more are the days that will calm
Our fears and our misgivings and work as a balm,
Bringing back memories of the good times we have had
Strengthening our hearts when we are alone and sad;

The days that are no more will be valued and preserved
For they hold in them that precious love that was served
Unconditionally, whether we deserved it or not
Even when we didn't reciprocate, neglected and forgot!

Those days that are no more are the days that will live on
Inspiring us to a better future, striving for a brighter dawn,
Teaching us to learn from our past follies and mistakes
Giving us comfort and soothing our heartaches!

*A line from Alfred, Lord Tennyson's 'The Princess: Tears, Idle Tears'

AND WHEN DO I REMEMBER?

And when do I
Remember you the most?
 ... When shadows lengthen
And cross the floor
From this window
To that far off door
And the sun is just preparing
To depart, taking with it
The warmth and the light
Ushering in a long dreary night;
When clouds gather
In great clusters ...
Threatening, hovering, circling,
But pass by and don't rain!

And when do I
Remember you the most?
 ... When the dove alights,
Perches, fluffs, muses and
Coos mournfully at my window
And abruptly flies away;
When the old melodious trilling
By that 'nightingale' of the east*
Suddenly lifts out and echoes
In the wilderness,
Shattering that heavy silence,
And infusing a sweet aching
Pathos all around;

And when do I
Remember you the most?
 ... When the moon glides up stealthily
Putting the stars to shame,

Mahmood Mustafa

Casting its soothing moonbeams
In all directions, unconditionally,
When the waters reflect and shimmer
Down the stream
 ... Silver flowing upon silver
 ... Uninterrupted!

That is when I remember you the most
And silently ...
Whisper your name!

....

'Nightingale' of the east* = The unparalleled, all-time great Indian female vocalist Lata Mangeshkar

BEYOND 150 AND BEAUTIFUL[*]

From BC[1] to Nova Scotia
From the great white tundra
To the southern fringes of Ontario ...
Canada, you are beautiful!

Dressed in the best
That nature can offer ...
Breathtaking mountains,
Crystal lakes and rolling prairies,
Scented pine forests and historic falls
Unique birds and rare animals ...
You stand unparallel!
Canada, you are beautiful!

How fortunate are we
To carry the Maple Leaf[2],
To wear your colours,
To sing your song
To move about with
Freedom, complete and total,
And also to practice and preach
Liberty and love and the varied beliefs ...
Unhindered but with discretion!
Canada, you are beautiful!

True, we come from far off lands
Different in colour and even in creed,
We bring with us varied cultures
And pour the goodness in the bigger bowl.
How can we give up our origin and roots?
How can we forget the beginnings?
If those were the mothers, so many of them,
They shall always be there for us,
But Canada... you are, for all, the true Godmother

Mahmood Mustafa

And you are beautiful!
Long live our land,
Long live our home
Long live Canada ...
We are proud and robust,
We celebrate you ...
From coast to coast,
Canada tu es belle!

---

*This poem was written in 2017 as Canada was celebrating its 150th anniversary of Confederation.
[1]British Columbia
[2]The flag of Canada (French: le drapeau du Canada), often referred to as the Canadian flag, or unofficially as the Maple Leaf and l'Unifolié (French for "the one-leafed")

A LONG WAY TO GO

Like the sun, unbiased, unconcerned,
Dispersing its warmth and sunlight
On all ... equally, unconditionally,
No specials, no favourites, no elites,
From land to sea, from field to hill
From forest to desert;

Like the flower, unselfish, impartial,
Blossoming and sharing
Its beauty and fragrance
Without fear or favour,
Not just with its neighbour
But to the whole garden and beyond ...

And there blows the wind
Ushering in the promise of new hope
Cooling and refreshing the land,
Bringing joy and hope
Steering rain-laden clouds
To parched fields ... unmarked, unnamed!

And there falls the rain
Unprejudiced, full of mercy,
Pure and clean,
Nourishing and restoring
The highs and lows ...
Rejuvenating life itself ... for all;

And here comes man,
'Indeed, created in the best of moulds,'
Centuries old
Yet in his nascent stage,
Uncouth, egotistical, jealous,

Mahmood Mustafa

Mean, suspicious, callous ...
Trouble and mischief on land and sea,
Trouble and mischief in air ...
From head to foot a persona of ...
Selfishness!

Still volumes to learn,
Still much to realize,
A very long journey to cover
Before ...
'Humans become humane'!

ONE DAY, SOMEDAY

Someday ...
It was going to be one day,
That one day, that someday,
Was going to be 'the' day ...
When the day would be seized
When it was going to be done
When everything would be set right
When all would be accomplished;
That one day, that someday!

Countless days have come
And countless days have gone
But that one day hasn't emerged
That someday hasn't arrived;
That one day,
That priceless day,
The chosen day
For which this 'defer plan' was invented ...
When it would be done
When it would be accomplished ...
Never transpired!

Was that day yesterday
Or one of the days before?
It can't be tomorrow
For where is tomorrow?
Who has seen tomorrow?
Could that one day,
Could that someday be today?
The only day we have seen
The only day we are alive
The only day we have been granted!

Mahmood Mustafa

THE MYSTIC SAGE

Building castles in the sand ...
Beautiful, attractive, charming
Castles in the sand
And selling them for a price that
All and sundry could afford
But along with a pledge few could buy
"Come own a castle in Paradise;"

Bahlul*, the mystic sage,
Sat on the beach as he would everyday,
Building sand castles of all shapes and sizes
Alluring curious passersby
Into buying a home in Paradise,
The faithful believed
The doubters heckled!
And as the day drew to a close
The sage dispensed all his hard-earned proceeds
Amongst the poor and the needy ...
The real purpose of this bizarre sale!

Out one evening came the royal entourage
Horses, elephants, soldiers and courtiers,
Smart in order, riches all around
And in the centre, in a dazzling display,
Harun al-Rashid himself, the Caliph of Arabian Nights;
As affluence paraded grandly by
Austerity, in stark contrast, toiled,
On the beach, Bahlul's dexterous fingers
Kept busy building more
Dream homes in Paradise.

Harun stopped amiably and inquired
"What is that you build with that paltry sand"?
"Castles in Paradise," replied Bahlul,
"O really? And are they for sale?" joked the Caliph,
"Yes, they are, want to buy one?"
"Sure," laughed the king, "and what is the price?"
"Only 10 dinars," said Bahlul softly;
"10 dinars for a sand castle? That is too expensive,"
Jeered the Caliph and moved on.
His laughter and jeering rang in the air.
But at the back of the entourage
Zubaidah, the wife of the caliph,
Heard the conversation and asked:
"Can I buy a home in Paradise, Bahlul?"
"Sure," said the sage "here is your castle,"
"And here is the value for the sale."
Zubaidah immediately offered the money.
Satisfied, she went home and Bahlul
Continued with his mysterios handiwork;

Soon the sun went down and night descended on Baghdad,
The palace went to sleep, the courtiers went to sleep,
The Caliph and his wife went to sleep, and the city went to sleep;
On that peaceful, balmy night, deep in slumber
The Caliph witnessed a scene like none before,

Mahmood Mustafa

He saw he had stumbled into a fascinating world,
In the most splendid surroundings,
A truly heavenly abode …
With crystal clear ponds, spectacular gardens,
Rivers of milk and honey,
Exquisite birds and flowers of rare fragrance
 … unbelievable ambience,
Dotted on all sides of the hills and plains
Between rolling velvety, smooth pastures,
Stood the most opulent
And luxurious castles and mansions
That even his kingdom hadn't seen or possessed,
All structures were seven stories high
And made of coloured jewels and decorated in grand style.
Weary and longing for rest, Harun's eye surveyed the scene
And settled on the most beautiful castle
And then he saw the extraordinary name on the gate,
The Caliph was blown away,
Engraved in gold the letters read "Zubaidah bint Ja'far,"
The Caliph, both shocked and happy,
Proudly strode up to the front door to enter,
But was served with a rude shock,
The guards stopped him, refusing entry,
He protested, insisting Zubaidah was his wife,
They were aware of it yet turned him away saying
"This castle is for Zubaidah, she earned it, none enters except her."
Dejected, disappointed, humiliated, as Harun was walking away
He woke up, perspiring, shaking and stunned,
He shot out of bed and paced the floor
For the remaining, 'unending' hours of the night
And at the first crack of dawn, Harun was away,
Galloping madly in pursuit of Bahlul …
Searching, stopping, checking all the haunts
That the sage would frequent, the Caliph finally found him …
In a new location, in a new mood,

The Bridge and The Bend

In a new 'bazaar' … hot on sale,
But with the same old wares!

"Bahlul," sighed Harun, relieved, "still building and selling castles in Paradise?"
"Very much so," retorted Bahlul, with a twinkle in his eyes,
"Why ask, interested in buying a palace in the stars?"
"Yes," enthused Harun, "right away, and here are your 10 dinars."
"No," challenged Bahlul, "the price today has seen a change."
"Really, and how much, may I ask is now the range?"
"The tag reads: Half your kingdom," the sage informed,
"Wha …t, half my kingdom, why, it was only 10 dinars?" the Caliph stormed.

"Simple my friend," explained Bahlul in a voice loud and clear,
As the Caliph stood helpless, shocked and in fear,
"That price yesterday was for customers who had
Believed and purchased, without seeing the reward,
But the rate today is for a trader who was not so keen,
And has only returned having witnessed the 'unseen'!"

The faithful, the ultimate winners, hear and obey;
The skeptics, may be, after they see and survey!
The wealth of the unseen is reward for belief,
And 'belief' must be implicit … anything less is grief!

Bahlūl (Arabic: بهلول) was the common name of Wāhab ibn Amr (Arabic: واهب ابن عمر), a companion of a famous religious leader and scholar. He lived in Baghdad (Iraq) in the time of the Caliph Hārūn al-Rashīd. Wāhab was a well-known judge and scholar who came from a wealthy background. He left his wealthy life, took to wearing rags and came into the streets and became a mystic saint. Baghdadis soon dubbed him Bahlūl (meaning foolish, stupid) but, ironically, they also called him 'Dana' meaning wise and intelligent.

Mahmood Mustafa

CALL FROM THE PAST

And now as I turn and look back
At the decades of sand and dust ...
No footprints, no markers,
No signposts, no reminders ...
From where I left
To where I headed,
And you didn't even call
For me to stop!

And then, suddenly,
I run into you ...
You stood there
Not the same anymore
A stranger ... trying to look away
Busying yourself with triviality
Pretending not to have seen,
But I caught your glance ...
It was the same
Though clouded with pain ...
Trying to hide, trying to disengage.
Four decades
Is a very long time,
In the interim ...
Many a bridge has collapsed,
Many a road has turned away,
Many a stream has meandered
Into oblivion, drying out,
Many a child has become a man
And many a man has left the stage!

The Bridge and The Bend

My head is silver and so is my face,
And furrows run deep across my brow
Reflecting the damage
Time has wreaked,
And I thought I caught signs of age
Around those lips too ...
Those very lips once so full
Of energy, love, life and mischief,
Always smiling, always teasing ...
Now seemed sad and quiet
And somewhat tired ...
Unlike in the past;

That was one strange encounter,
One alarming brush,
One roller-coaster memory jog ...
One sweet-bitter call from the past!

Mahmood Mustafa

COUCHICHING* REVISITED

With a few more years
Lapsing in the interim,
And a few more seasons,
Fleeting by ...
I revisit you
Couchiching ...
With summer still in its prime,
But with a difference ...
Bigger, larger patches of grey
Both in the head and the beard ...
A few more aches,
A few more pains in the joints!
But when I turn and
Look at you and your shoreline ...
Beautiful as ever
Young and youthful like before
Or even more splendid,
The water is as calm
And placid as before;
Gently, gracefully, languidly
Lapping on to the shore,
Movement but with grace,
Progress but with control ...
The playful little waves
Showing off as though
Big in strength and force
But gurgling, like tiny giggles,
Breaking against my feet.
The sky as blue as can be,
Clearly marking its boundary
Against the darker hue of Couchiching ...
Touching softly, lovingly,
Each seems to be making an effort

The Bridge and The Bend

To meet gently,
As though merging in one another,
Yet keeping the distance and not
Trespassing on privacy ...
Couchiching ...
Till the next time ...
Stay fresh and as always
..... Young and stunning!

....

Lake Couchiching, is situated in Central Ontario separated from Lake Simcoe by a narrow channel. The lake is 16 km long, slightly less than 5 km wide and fairly shallow. The city of Orillia is located on the narrow channel connecting this lake with Lake Simcoe. Lake Couchiching is a popular spot for fishing in summer and ice fishing in winter. In autumn the forests around the lake explode in unbelievable vibrant colours.

Mahmood Mustafa

MEVLANA, SALAAM

Mevlana[1] Salaam[2]; Mevlana Salaam,
The Teacher, the Master, the Guide,
... Salaam ...
Rumi[3] Salaam, Rumi Salaam!

Love, poesy, logic and devotion,
Music, mysticism, wisdom
And much more,
Gather at your doorstep
With folded hands
Standing in awe and respect,
Awaiting your command
To perform, to flow, to play
And gush forth and spread
In new directions!

Konya[4], that chosen land,
The land of mysticism,
The land of culture,
The seat of knowledge
Host and home to the gracious Master
And his teachings
Spanning over eight centuries ...
To you Konya ... Salaam!

I come to you O gentle city,
And I come to you O learned Master,
I sit at your feet
In quest of learning
In quest of knowledge,
In quest of wisdom,
My pen is thirsty,
My pen is restless,

Impatient to compose
Anxious to write ...
Let the ink flow, fill me
With your mystic colours,
Let my thoughts surrender to yours,
And let your insight infuse mine,
Let your spirit ignite my soul
And let that fusion erupt
In a new exemplary ballad,
In an unsung melody,
In fresh, unsaid lyrics,
And flow through my pen ...
And let that 'Derveshi'[5] song
Echo eternally!

Tomb of mystic poet/saint Jalaluddin Muhammad Rumi in Konya, Turkey - Photo credit: Mahmood Mustafa

[1]*Mevlana: Master (Rumi, the mystic poet/saint as referred to)*
[2]*Salaam: a salutation meaning "peace;" salutation, salute*
[3]*Rumi: The Turkish poet and mystic Jalaluddin Muhammad Rumi*
[4]*Konya: A town in Turkey, where the sufi saint Rumi lived and is buried*
[5]*Derveshi: From the word 'Dervish': a member of a religious order noted for devotional bodily movements leading to a trance.*

Mahmood Mustafa

THOSE SUFI[1] DAYS

To be where the Sufi[1] is,
Is the yearning and desire,
The home and hearth of bliss
The eternal flame and fire;

Blessed were they who shared
Those times and days with you[2]
Together they lived and prayed
And soaked that wisdom new;

To see the Master[3] twirl
To hear the Master play
His magic reed and unfurl
Those longing arms each day;

Trivial moments sometimes go
With memories sewed to them
Tiny raindrops often flow
With rainbows glued to them;

One journey, one passage, one visit
Is not enough the thirst to quench,
The longing to return, to revisit,
Is deep in the heart entrenched

Some day with grace from above,
I shall return to you and your love!

Photo courtesy: unsplash.com

[1]*Sufi: A follower of Sufism, mystical belief and practice in which the sufi devotee seeks to find the truth of divine love and knowledge through direct personal experience of God.*
[2]*You: Jalaluddin Mohammad Rumi, the mystic poet/saint*
[3]*Master (Rumi, the mystic poet/saint as referred to)*

DRIVE TO SQUAMISH (BC)

Eyes, like cameras,
Busy clicking and capturing
Scenes unparalleled, indescribable,
And the winding road
Kept throwing surprises
At bends with unrivalled beauty;

The snow-clad mountains
In the distant horizon,
Like sages with silver locks
Having witnessed uncountable eons,
Having presided over eras
Immeasurable,
Look down upon the ocean
Of insignificant bodies
Darting to and fro
Trying to soak up
Years of history
In just a few puffs of breath,
..... Borrowed breaths; fleeting breaths ...
To vainly display on their lapels
These rare adventures
To those unfortunates
Who were not blessed
With these treasures, this rare opportunity ...
Either to possess
Or to witness.

We stop to catch our breaths
And a bite,
To trek along in the thicket
And refresh ourselves in the gentle spray
Of Shannon Falls, tumbling and falling

Mahmood Mustafa

Hundreds of meters,
Bringing fresh filtered water;
Here at this bend
I look up and catch the sheer blue of the sky
And again from the same spot
I change my gaze and
Look down to catch another blue ...
But this time it is hundreds of feet below ...
The blue of the sea.
And true to its name ...
It is a Sea-to-Sky-highway!

And just a short distance away
The granite cliffs and the bluffs,
Present a strange commotion below,
And as the climb continues upwards
The fairy-tale beauty keeps unraveling
And in one small dish of the eye,
At different angles,
You catch and soak the breathtaking splendour ...
Squamish, you and your winding trails,
Are simply humbling!

....

Squamish is a town north of Vancouver, in British Columbia, Canada. It's at the northern tip of the island-dotted Howe Sound, and surrounded by mountains like the Stawamus Chief, a huge granite monolith. Squamish is ideally situated on the scenic Sea to Sky Highway between Vancouver, British Columbia's largest city and Whistler, a four-season mountain resort consistently ranked the number one ski resort in North America. The Sea to Sky Gondola has views of the sound and nearby Shannon Falls, a towering waterfall cascading down a series of cliffs. The Britannia Mine Museum has underground train tours. Bike trails criss-cross the area. Located at the northern tip of a glacially etched fjord on the Pacific Ocean, surrounded by a spectacular mountain backdrop and nestled within a temperate rainforest, Squamish is recognized worldwide for its culture, recreation and incredible mountain lifestyle.
Source: © 2019. District of Squamish, British Columbia.

AND ALL AT ONCE ...

"And all at once,
Summer collapsed into fall"*
And music that was heard ...
All through
Those arresting warm months ...
Began to fade
From reeds and pipes hidden
In the trunks of trees;
And streams and ponds
That sang familiar themes
And the symphony which
Echoed from vale to hill,
Also quietened down ...
Reluctantly!

But in the meantime,
A riot broke out in the garden,
Down the track
And the field beyond,
With gold vying with magenta
And red competing with yellow,
And the hills turning multi-coloured too
And the delicate spread
Taking on a richer, toasted brown hue ...
Harvest was ready!

The wind also began altering its tune ...
From a gentle hum to
A cool, shrill whistle,
And the air seemed a little heavy
With smoke and mist
Hanging suspended for longer spells,
Unwillingly,

Mahmood Mustafa

Unsure of the direction to take!
Autumn had arrived ...
With its varied and countless
Shades of colours,
Its falling leaves like sparks
From a Victoria Day shindig
And the foliage changing quick tones ...
Now green, now yellow, now purple, now brown!

Autumn, preparing nature to shed the old
And wait till new spring attires arrive,
And also scurrying little creatures along
To store big supplies .....
Autumn ...
The forerunner of Winter ...
Has arrived!

"And all at once, summer collapsed into fall" ... A line from Oscar Wilde

THE AWAKENING

How and where
Do people get the time
To offer hatred,
Hand out remorse,
Distribute spite
Deliver pain
Carry malice and dole out discomfort?
When here,
There is hardly any time
To give and get love,
To hug away all misunderstandings,
To clear the path of stones and thorns
Even for that stranger,
The stranger that I know not and
Who does not recognize me,
So that he can walk in comfort,
In safety and in peace
And does not stumble and fall
Or bleed or be hurt!

And how and where do they get the time
To love with a purpose
To care with a reason
To give with a motive
To cry with an aim?
When life, that passing shadow,
Is hardly catchable
Or in any way stoppable,
But is the perfect lesson
In melt, fleet and spent ...

One realization, one awakening,
One truth, can transform
The entire mindset ...
From charade to honesty!

Mahmood Mustafa

THE BRIDGE AND THE BEND

How many bridges have I crossed
In my lifetime?
Thousands, perhaps …
Some low, some high,
Some broad, some narrow,
Some leading to greenery and pastures,
Some heading straight into ghost towns,
Some keeping me at the edge of my seat
And some lulling me to sleep …

In this chequered journey,
How many bends have I turned?
Countless …
Some sharp, some curved,
Some smooth, some rough …
Bends sloping down dangerously,
Bends rising uphill suddenly,
Some coming to an abrupt end
And some merging into unending highways …

But no bridge, no bend has left
Its mark, its impression,
Etched in memory …
As that one bridge and that one bend …
The bridge where I met you for the first time
And the bend where I lost you forever!

THE GOLDEN CHRONICLES

Like yesterday,
And the many fleeting days
That have slipped away
And become yesteryears
In succession ... never to return,
Life moves on ...
Helpless and incapable
Of hugging or holding
Or bringing them
Or other realities back which have,
Unknowingly, silently, achingly,
Vanished into the past.

The pace has been,
And is,
Incredibly swift,
Hardly pausing to glance back
To recollect, to recount
To measure the depth
And intensity of it all ...

But there has been one source,
One narrative, one witness
That survives and lives on
With passion and pain
Trying desperately to hold
And keep alive the past ...
Both golden and bloody ...
And with it the many truths,
The many forgotten names
The countless faces now blurred,
Those significant sites,
Those momentous events

That deserve mention
That shout out for recognition,
And those not so rosy years
Nor pleasant personalities ...
In fact dark and tyrannical,
But utterly necessary to remember
So they are not repeated
Or mislead future generations ...

Yes ...
And that one tireless source,
That one busy narrator, one honest witness
That has survived and lives on
With passion and pain,
Desperately trying to hold
Mirror to time and events
Has been none other
Than the great recorder
 ... History!

FOOTPRINTS IN THE SKY

How come?
The stars and the Milky Way
Seem to sparkle and glisten
With such brilliance,
Such freshness, so luminous,
Even after eons in orbit,
Centuries of voyage
Colossal upheavals,
Countless births,
Innumerable rebirths and deaths,
Yet there seems to be
A permanent glow,
A velvety, rich light ...
So pure and unmatched,
So fresh in the cosmos!

Could this be the
Bounty of some
Divine, blessed feet
As they ascended stairways
Of unimaginable radiance,
And as they travelled on
Bolts of lightning,
On an Unprecedented journey,
Crossing the utmost periphery
Of time, space and energy
To unexplainable destinations
For classified mystic meetings
For the salvation and glory of Humankind?

Shrouded in mystery
The night and the passage,
The carriers and the ascender
The purpose and the outcome!

Mahmood Mustafa

TO MY GOOD FRIEND 'B' ...

Courage, patience and hope
Are the only pillars one can
Lean on to garner strength
And continue on the journey of life;

How easy come the words
Of consoling and counseling,
How tough it is to feel the pain
And live somebody else's sorrow;

Life throws up strange patterns
And presents stranger paradoxes,
Some almost predictable
Some utter bolts from the blue;

But resilience, endurance and fortitude
Have won many a daunting battle,
And you, my dear, have always shown
What it takes to stand up, smile and prevail!

THE JOURNEY CONTINUES

Dawn, the infant dawn,
Quickly budding
And growing into that youthful day,
Taking advantage of the light,
Has repeatedly
Raced the course ...
The entire course,
From east to west ...
In search of you,
Restless!

At times gray and sad,
At times slow and lethargic
But mostly swift and sudden ...
It has done the course,
The entire course,
In search of you!

And each time that it has
Met dusk, faithfully,
It has inquired and sought news
Of you, searching and
Seeking your whereabouts,

Unsuccessful so far,
The journey continues ...
The search is on ...
For you!

PS: Talash mey hai sahar bar bar guzri hai (The dawn is in search and has repeatedly passed by) ... Faiz Ahmed Faiz

Mahmood Mustafa

AND HOW MANY WILL YOU DENY?

How can you count your myriad blessings,
Who in this world can do that count?
Try denying them or even better, guessing,
And see how quickly those numbers mount;

And how many of them will you deny?
And how many of them will you deny?

Your speech, your hearing, your intelligence,
The computed courses of the sun, the moon,
The herbs, the trees, the vast firmament,
Each a blessing, an unmatched boon;

The earth is alive and is perpetually growing
Grain and fruit and corn and fodder,
With sweet-smelling flowers gently blowing
And nature tasked with healing and order;

Then which of the blessings will you deny?
Then which of the favours will you deny?

Let's look east, let's look west, let's see all around,
The great expanse, the deep serene water
Where pearls and corals and treasures abound,
And the nights and days complement each other.

The ships, like lofty mountains, smoothly sail
And the unending skies majestically beckon
Man to fly out and of opportunities avail
And attain much more than he can reckon;

The Bridge and The Bend

Then which of the blessings will you deny?
Then which of the favours will you deny?
Worlds beyond this world have stood
Waiting with riches, promises of bliss
The reward of good is nothing but good
So strive and work for more than this;

The daily bread, the nightly sleep,
Our clothing and the security of roof,
Are gifts worthy of gratitude .... long and deep,
To be deemed as blessings, shown as proof.

Then which of the blessings will you deny?
Then which of the favours will you deny?

My tongue is tied, my mind goes blank
I struggle to think and search for expression,
To pick the courage, to count and thank
But failing, fall into utter depression,

Then which of the blessings should I deny?
Then which of the favours can I deny?

Mahmood Mustafa

IN MEMORIAM*

I stood there gazing
At you ...
Four decades had elapsed
Silently, unnoticed,
All occupants had left
Some never to return, some to drift away
To far off known, unknown lands,
Not intending to cross paths again
And even if they did ...
Only as strangers,
Pretending never to have met,
Silently ... choking, suffocating,
Swiping away tears ... in hiding
Lest the marks, the traces lead to
Days and years gone by ...
Days and tales best forgotten!

But you, '304'[1], have stood the test of time,
A citadel of love, hope and comfort,
When all tracks seemed to run to Stonebridge[2]
And all streets and pathways from there
Seemed to hurry to you ...
The great refuge, the haven, the platform
For many an unsure life
To take a chance, to launch,
To make a new beginning ...
And presiding over with their support, warmth,
Selfless service and love,
The two pillars[3] ... one with a mother's thoughtfulness
And the other with the guidance of a father ...
Who touched countless lives,
Mending, spending and fending to better them,
Bearing with patience the whims of the boisterous,

The Bridge and The Bend

Soothing and calming
The rile of the unreasonable!

Those towering figures,
At times seeming larger than reality,
Absorbing, bearing and tolerating
Without a whisper, for the sake of ties!
Always keeping the door open, unlocked,
The hearth warm and ready to welcome,
The table spread with food for the hungry
And not a question asked of any!

Happy and content,
There are countless ... some strangers ...
Now spread over the globe, flourishing,
Who owe it to them, their care and love,
Their goodness and patience and more,
Remembering them with smiling faces
Yet with eyes moist ...
Your memories are ever fresh ...
Fresh as the morning dew
And your names mentioned,
always, with reverence ...
Rest in peace ...
Angels of peace!

The house in Wembly, England

---

*Title borrowed from Alfred Lord Tennyson's great work
[1]304, a house in Wembley, England, where the poet had lived with his aunt and uncle.
This poem is a tribute to their memory, love, patience and benevolence.
[2] Stonebridge Park: a train station close to that house
[3]The aunt and uncle

Mahmood Mustafa

HOMEWARDS?

Am I who I am?
Are you the real you?
Could we just be shadows,
Silhouettes,
Being cast through a prism
From a distant, far off land ...
Extra-terrestrial ...
The real world, the real home?

Could we just be in transit,
On our way back
To reality,
To that everlasting abode ...
Momentarily losing focus,
Enchanted and sidetracked,
Trapped and just a little distracted
By the glitter of an alien land,
Losing direction?

The sooner the realization ...
The better;
The quicker the needle set on course ...
The safer,
For the 'call' from home
Could be on its way ...
Just around the corner....
Coming ...
To wake up, to energize ...
To exit,
And be transported!

HOPE AND FEAR

What is Faith?
The condition and emotion
Between Hope and Fear ...
Hoping for the best,
But always questioning
Your effort and labour,
And often fearing the result
May not be the best,
Always putting it to test
Lest pride and ego take over
And blind your vision
Making you live and believe
In falsehood
And you take your work
For granted and expect
Rewards and returns
Way above and beyond;

And when you know
You haven't done your very best,
In spite of all the hard work
The toil and the sweat,
You feel you may fall short
Of the expected bar
And may not accomplish
Or meet the required
Target that was set,
Then keep hope alive
And look to the brighter side,
If not all, some part of your labour
Might outstand the rest
And may be recognized
And you may still be rewarded for

Mahmood Mustafa

Something you never dreamed of!
To keep the boat of life steady
On the unsure stream of time,
Always look to the water and shore
With both hope and fear ...
And wisely ply the medium course!

IBADAH*

I sit with my eyes glued to your door,
A devotee in worship,
Wrapped in thoughts,
Where the mind begins
To pulsate and beat
Like the heart
And learns to hear and obey …
The voice within;

Where the gaze shifts not
And the focus moves not
And thoughts stray not,
If I can't see You …
You can,
If I can't get a glimpse
Of splendour,
So be it,
I am blessed, after all, to be viewing
Your door,
Your 'House,'
Beholding them is 'Ibadah'* in itself!

---

*Ibadah: Arabic word meaning worship, obedience, submission

Mahmood Mustafa

ELVEDA[1] TURKEY !

(This poem was written during an excursion to Turkey in 2017)

I

Elveda[1] Turkey!
Goodbye Turkey ...
As I stand alone on this terrace,
Up above this bustling global metro[2]
And as dusk settles into a peaceful night,
I look down at the breathtaking view
On my last evening of this sojourn
And recollect the sights,
The sounds, the fragrance,
The feel and the taste
Of those last few weeks ...
A calm sense of solace
Overtakes, encompassing me
In unexplainable moments of joy!

II

I look out over the rows of trees,
The neatly-lined rooftops
And the calm, tranquil water
And my eyes travel and take me
To the distant straits ..... Bosporus,[3]
And the twinkling lights from passing ships
And beyond to the other shore,
Where more lights twinkle and greet me!
Bosporus ... the bridge
Between the two great land masses,
Between the two great continents,
Also, the waterway, the lifeline, connecting
The Black Sea[4] to the Marmara[5];

III

Spreading over two vast regions
Of Europe and Asia,
Turkey, you are, at once, home
To two proud peoples
Boasting hundreds of cultures,
Customs, costumes and beliefs,
The rock-solid bond between
The East and the West,
The meaningful link
Between two opposite worlds!
You, that historical beacon,
That critical lighthouse
To millions on either side
Of the divide ...
A divide which in reality
Joins millions of hearts, minds and hands,
Rather than separates!

Below: Bosporus straits
Photo credit: Mahmood Mustafa

IV

Turkey, the great maker and recorder of history,
In your lap were born and flourished
The most magnificent and durable
Empires and emperors of humankind,
You, the witness to timeless legends and
Unforgettable names,
The preserver of traditions,
Unique and distinct cultures
And memorable and priceless monuments ...
From Topkapi[6] to the Blue Mosque[7]
To Hagia Sophia[8], where the Holy Mother
To this day presides and looks down
With love and care at all her children!
Turkey ... where history joins hands with
Geography and delivers a sermon to religion
On tolerance and camaraderie,
Where churches, mosques and synagogues
Are alive and serve and exist
In brotherly neighbourhoods,
Where peace dwells languidly and cements
Age-old ties of friendship, unity and patience!

Right: The Blue Mosque
Photo courtesy: unsplash.com

V

You, the cradle of civilizations,
Home to great prophets,
Saints, sages, mystics and poets,
With messages of hope
And teachings of love for
The whole of mankind;
Where Rumi[9] still twirls in the
Circles of peace,
In the bazaars of grace
And is sung and heard
From Istanbul to the sky-scraping
Mount Ararat[10] in the east!

VI

O beloved city! O beloved nation,
Turkey, I stand here tonight,
To salute you and your glorious past ...
A past that proudly stands on
Thousands of golden annals ...
I salute all those great empires,
I salute all those great religions,
I salute all the great legends
Who nourished and nurtured
You with sweat and blood ...
Gave you love and gave you life ...
To make you what you are today.
I stand here and gaze at the bright shining stars
And make a small prayer for you ... Turkey,
May you be protected,
And may you, your cultures, your history
Live on to be preserved
And guarded for posterity,
May you flourish, flower and prosper

Mahmood Mustafa

For generations to profit,
For your treasures are treasures
Of the world ...
A universal heritage and legacy!
Yaşasın[11] Turkey!
Yaşasın Turkey!

Right: Turkey at night
Photo courtesy: unsplash.com

[1] *Elveda: Turkish word meaning: Goodbye*
[2] *Global metro: Istanbul*
[3] *Bosporus: The Bosporus, also known as The Strait of Istanbul, is a narrow, natural strait and an internationally significant waterway located in northwestern Turkey. It forms part of the continental boundary between Europe and Asia. The world's narrowest strait used for international navigation, the Bosporus connects the Black Sea with the Sea of Marmara.*
[4] *Black Sea: The Black Sea is a body of water and marginal sea of the Atlantic Ocean between Eastern Europe, the Caucasus, and Western Asia.*
[5] *Marmara: The Sea of Marmara, also known as the Marmara Sea, is a small sea, entirely within the borders of Turkey, which connects the Black Sea to the Aegean Sea, thus separating Turkey's Asian and European parts.*
[6] *Topkapi: The Topkapi Palace, or the Seraglio, is a large museum in Istanbul. In the 15th century, it served as the main residence and administrative headquarters of the Ottoman sultans.*
[7] *The Blue Mosque: The Sultan Ahmed Mosque (also known as the Blue Mosque) is a historic mosque located in Istanbul. It remains a functioning mosque, while also attracting large numbers of tourist visitors. Hand-painted blue tiles adorn the mosque's interior walls (hence Blue Mosque).*
[8] *Hagia Sophia is the former Greek Orthodox Christian patriarchal cathedral, and now a museum (Ayasofya Müzesi) in Istanbul. Built in AD 537 at the beginning of the Middle Ages, it was famous in particular for its massive dome.*
[9] *Rumi: Jalāluddin Muhammad Rūmī was a 13th-century Persian poet, Islamic scholar, theologian, and Sufi mystic originally from Greater Khorasan. He lived and is buried in Konya, Turkey.*
[10] *Mount Ararat: Mount Ararat is a snow-capped and dormant compound volcano in the extreme east of Turkey. It consists of two major volcanic cones: Greater Ararat and Little Ararat*
[11] *Yaşasın: Turkish word meaning: Hooray, long live, thumbs up, hip hip hooray!*

LONE AUDIENCE

Dusk ...
A few puffs of clouds,
The East
... A silver spread,
The Moon
 ... A half-filled bowl above the horizon
The West
.... A concave screen splashed in colours
And I
 ... The lone audience!

Mahmood Mustafa

PERPETUITY

Sitting by this ocean, vast,
At the foot of the mighty Rockies,
On the edge of this wide, rolling landscape
And glancing up at the unending sky ...
I pause to think
Dear Friend, of You
And your limitless mercy,
Your lavish care
Your boundless benevolence
Your profundity to forgive,
Forget and put up with,
And your presence
There and here ...
From eternity to infinity ...
Omnipotent!

On the flip side:
A few countable breaths
A few measured and stray steps
A few numbered days
A few 'boastful' victories
A few scalable heights
A few shallow gains ...
And man ... the mortal ... loses his equilibrium,
Loses control and focus
Gloats and floats all around
And does not fail to impress and brag,
With the spotlight never failing to shift
From 'I, me and myself'!

Little me, little you,
Little I, little us,
Little myself and little ourselves

Little all ...
Momentary, brief, passing,
Transitory, fleeting, short-lived;
All this explains and provides ...
Proof and meaning of:
Temporary, fragile and perishable
And again, on the flip side:
Perpetuity!

Mahmood Mustafa

IQBAL'S[1] MESSAGE

"Forbear the goblet, abandon comfort
Because life is not for drowsy sleep,
Summon the caravan, take the road
Now time is ripe, now harvest reap!

Weep not if one world is lost from sight
Save your breath for unconquered lands,
Your Khudi[2] is strength, your faith a light
So pluck the stars with your mighty hands!

Your task is flight for a falcon you are
And many a blue is spread for you,
Your destiny is you and not a star
So shatter this myth, this pagan view!

Here destiny is carved in accordance with will
So leave not your fortune to another hand,
The subjects of fate are this tree, that hill
You were born to obey the Holy command,"

So uttered the saint a message divine
A message so true and for every ear,
But today it is wealth, women and wine ...
A falcon, alas, has turned into a vulture!

---

[1] Sir Dr. Muhammad Iqbal (November 9, 1877 – April 21, 1938), widely known as Allama Iqbal (Allama is an honorary title for scholars of Islamic fiqh [jurisprudence]and philosophy), was a poet, philosopher, politician, academic, barrister and scholar in British-occupied India. He is considered an important figure in Urdu literature, with literary works in both Urdu and Persian. Though Iqbal is best known as an eminent poet, he is also an acclaimed "Muslim philosophical thinker of modern times" and is widely regarded as having inspired the Pakistan Movement. Along with his Urdu and Persian poetry, his Urdu and English lectures and letters have been very influential in cultural, social, religious and political disputes. In the 1923 New Years Honours he was made a Knight Bachelor by King George V, while studying law and philosophy in England. — Source: Wikipedia

[2] Khudi: Urdu word meaning: Self, ego (in the positive sense); self-confidence, self-assertion, self-esteem and self-recognition

PATTERNS

Shadows
Across my bed,
Across the carpet,
Chequered shadows
Across the room
Form long, slanting
And uneven
Patterns ...
So much like
Life itself!

Mahmood Mustafa

IT IS ... NOW!

And so I met this sage
In the market place
Standing in a corner
With a drooping head,
Leaning on his staff,
Dejected and sad,
He wept and continued weeping,
As I quizzed him
And asked about his woe,
The reason, the source of his anguish,
He raised his head,
That wise silver head,
And sighed:
"I offered to make peace
Between them and Him" – looking up at the sky!
"But they declined and laughed,
Said they were busy, a life had to be lived,
So much to do, so many chores,
So where was the time for all of this?
That makes me shudder,
That makes me cry"!

The next day,
I saw the same old man,
This time by the cemetery,
The same drooping head,
The same dejection and sadness,
Leaning on his staff
Weeping and much more!
I asked him "old man,
What is with you?
Yesterday it was the hectic marketplace,
Today it is this silent cemetery ...

And again those tears?"
He looked up at me
With a distant gaze, shook his head and said:
"It is a similar story friend:
Yesterday He was willing" pointing to the sky,
"They didn't have time,
And today" pointing to the graves
"They are willing and have time,
But He, unhappy and displeased,
Has turned away"!

Alive is hope ... dead is done,
If not today ... then tell me when?

Mahmood Mustafa

WIND IN THE WILDERNESS

The wind,
Wearing tiny trinkets,
Danced on my window sill ...
All night long,
The rain kept alive its gentle patter
And the wet leaves,
Soaked and heavy,
Hummed yawny, lazy melodies,
Lulling the world to sleep
But I kept awake,
Trapped in the webs of
The past and you ...
All night long!

The hands
Had done their rounds, several,
And returned to the beginning
 ... A huge passage ...
And the face of the clock
Looked tired and sullen
As I sat wide-eyed
Till the rays began filtering
Through the rustling trees ...
Much like pure milk through a strainer,
Darkness playing
Hide and seek with fresh emerging light ...

All night the tempo was up ...
The wind, the rain, the leaves,
The rustling and I
Stayed awake till dawn ...
Till the Muezzin[1], finally,
Called out to the faithful

From the minaret²,
To come join the ranks in worship,
And that is when, surprisingly,
The wind eased off
And gradually died,
And I, so tired and worn,
Went back to join
The unforgiving day!

---

¹Muezzin = A man who calls the faithful to prayer
²Minaret = A tall slender tower, typically part of a mosque, with a balcony from which the muezzin calls for prayer.

Mahmood Mustafa

A NEW JOURNEY

Night ...
Silence, stillness and calm,
And far in the distance
I hear
Wheels beginning to roll ...
A little huff and a chuff
A lone whistle,
Shattering the peace,
Signaling the start
Of a new journey
In a new, unknown direction,
Up against new challenges,
New obstacles,
Crossing unseen bridges,
Streaking across fields and meadows,
Cutting across dark and deep forests,
Scaling new mountains,
Negotiating dark tunnels
Rushing by unimportant, insignificant stations,
Not stopping,
Aiming and focusing only
On the final destination ...

And close by in the neighbourhood
I hear the tiny snivel,
The helpless, weak cry
Of a newborn,
And again the stillness breaks,
The silence and the calm are disturbed
Signaling the start
Of another new journey ...
A similar yet ... a different journey ...
A sacred and precious journey,
A pristine journey ... Viva life!

LUQMAN*, TO THE PROGENY

The earth is a carpet spread out for us,
Today it is under our careless feet
And we tread on it,
But tomorrow when we are done,
We go under, beneath it ...
Helpless and spent,
So use it gently and walk with humbleness,
Always keep the end in mind,
Hear and take heed to what Luqman*,
The wise man, said to his son
Centuries ago,
And ponder on it,
Both as advice and warning:

"False worship, indeed, is the highest wrong,
A very grave injustice,
So join not others, O my son;
Establish regular prayer,
Enjoin what is good, what is just,
And forbid what is wrong and evil;
Bear with patience whatever
Sufferings befall and touch you,
For this is firmness of purpose,
Matters of great courage and resolve,
And purchase not idle tales
Without knowledge or meaning.
Swell not your cheek in pride at men
Or turn your face away
From the public in arrogance,
Nor walk in insolence and self-conceit
Through the earth,
For an arrogant boaster is never loved
Nor succeeds;

Mahmood Mustafa

Be moderate, my son, in your pace
And lower your voice,
For the harshest of sounds, without doubt,
Is the braying of the donkey"!

So advised the sage:
Prayer, righteousness, courage,
Humbleness and moderation
Are pillars that wise lives lean on
To transcend from worthless ranks
To unparalleled excellence!

---

*Luqman (also known as Luqman the Wise, Luqmaan, Lukman, and Luqman al-Hakeem; Arabic: لقمان) was a wise man. Luqman (c. 1100 BC) is believed to be from Ethiopia. There are many stories about Luqman in Persian, Arabic and Turkish literature. The Bahá'í holy writings also make reference to Luqman. Luqman was described as a perceptive man, always watching the animals and plants of his surroundings, and he tried to understand the world based on what he saw.— Wikipedia

PERCEPTIONS

When you were young
And I was young
And the world was a lot younger;
When the sun seemed
A little brighter
And the night a little
More charming;
When those feet were much nimbler
And our hearts a little lighter ...

It was a beautiful world!
It was a young world,
A different world,
A friendlier and richer world ...
And it was our world!

But really?
Was the world younger?
Was the world different?
Was it friendlier and richer?
Was the world beautiful?
Or ...
Was all this
Just ... us?

A different world?
Yes, where we fit in very well
As we were part of it then,
Today when we
Do not alter and adjust
It seems a strange world
And not our world;

Mahmood Mustafa

More than the eye
Beauty lies in the mind
And our attitude,
Keep the mind and attitude young
And the world stays young ...
Forever!

REMEMBER ME

The deal is simple:
'You remember me and
I will remember you'!
Remembrance also
Calls for thankfulness
And not rejecting
The giver, the patron
The provider!

Remembrance and
Acknowledgement
Keep you in focus,
In the sight and thoughts of
Him, who matters,
Always multiplying love,
Piety and kindness,
Increasing bounties manifold!

Thankfulness is also
The door to humbleness,
Cleansing one from
Pride and egotism,
Learning to give and share,
When needed being there!

Remember to be remembered,
Serve to be served!

Mahmood Mustafa

KAVANAH*

Long silky robes,
Hands and neck decked
In colourful beads,
Locks swaying, in vanity,
On decorated shoulders,
And the proud beard
Impressive and flowing;
Rosary to busy the fingers,
Studded with colorful gems ...
Without ... striking adornments,
Within ... very little 'Kavanah'!

He walks around with his cavalcade
To mesmerize humanity,
And most fall for it,
Putting this 'diviner' on high ground,
Kissing his hands, kissing his robes,
Sitting at his feet ...
Within ... very little 'Kavanah.'

And his community is large
All over the globe, ready, on hand,
Representing all faiths, all creeds,
Trading with the poor, the helpless,
Cashing in on their innocence,
Cashing in on ignorance!

But the mirror laughs,
The mirror mocks,
It can see through,
It knows the truth!
So short a journey and such big a fraud?
The scales will soon be erected,

They will stand tall and in public,
Only 'Kavanah' will then be weighed,
Measured and tested,
Only 'Neeyat' will then be computed and counted,
And then:
An eternally distressing verdict!

*Hebrew word: meaning sincere intention. In Arabic/Urdu: Niyyah/Neeyat

Mahmood Mustafa

REMEMBRANCE

When in these eyes your vision appears
All clothed in love yet damped by tears,
Long, slumbering memories rise to pain
This heart, this mind, this soul again!

When in this mind your thoughts arise
Ushering the past merged in sighs,
Hazy recollections worsen my soul
Forcing warm tears to roll;

When to my heart your pain returns
And your past company when it yearns,
No humble comfort seems to rush
To me, a few tears to brush;

The thirst in my soul shall never be quenched
Although my eyes seem ever drenched!

SANS WINTER

Who would have
Treasured spring
Or waited patiently
For that glorious summer
Or for the colour riot to break down the valley,
In gardens, in backyards and in flowerbeds;
For the sky to turn blue
Or the brook to flow a healthier width?
Who would have waited
To hear the robin sing
And the dove to melodiously moan
As the sultry noon hours
Laze in thick, soft, sleepy shadows,
Who would ... without winter?

But wake, for it is still biting out there!
It is still that white blanket
Covering land and hill!
It is still gray and sad in the sky
The trees still stand shivering,
Naked and bare,
The wind is still a chilling arrow
And the only semblance of clothing
Is hope,
But ...
If Winter comes, can Spring be far behind?*

If Winter comes, can Spring be far behind?
From: An Ode to The West Wind by Percy Bysshe Shelley

Mahmood Mustafa

THE BELOVED OF ALL

How should I say?
What can I say?
And what must I say ...
Mercy for all, Mercy for all!

You lift your eyes
Those beautiful eyes,
Those lustrous eyes,
Those gracious eyes ...
Mercy for all, Mercy for all!

You part your lips,
Those delicate petals
Imparting wisdom, rare,
Delivering gems, priceless,
Mercy for all, Mercy for all!

That smile ... warm, genuine,
Captivating, mesmerizing,
Comforting, beneficial,
That life-giving remedy,
Mercy for all, Mercy for all!

Beloved of all,
Like moths circling around
The flame, seeking to enter
And burn in that glorious glow ...
So do the devotees,
Hover around
Ready to perish and find
Everlasting existence;
Salutations to you,
Mercy for all, Mercy for all!

BAY OF FUNDY

Where the tide recedes
Miles into the distant horizon ...
Deep into the ocean's bosom,
Leaving the shore and its bed
And all that it had covered
Bare ...
Exposing the earth, the shells
And vegetation which
Is hard to guess existed
Beneath;
What had been a
Basin filled with water
Is now empty ...
Empty and bare ...
As though giant hands had got hold of
A giant bucket,
Clutched it at the mouth and bottom
And flung the water
Far out there in the distance ...

And when the tide returns,
Bringing back
Tons of fresh water,
Submerging a whole visible world,
Giant rocks, beside which man stands a pigmy,
Vanish,
Plants and shrubs, where we had run and rested,
Laying mats upon the ground,
And ate and picnicked all day,
Disappear within hours
And the tips of some tops
Are visible only as blades of grass
After a lawn had been mowed,

With rafts and boats plying
And fish and humans swimming once again ...
As though this was always an 'aqua home,'
A tub filled with water!

And what did the Bay tell me,
What message did it convey?

This is what life is all about,
This is how life should be lived ...
This is the way to conduct your affairs ...
Ebb with the tide
And flow with the surge ...
Bend, blow and survive
Stand stiff, resist and break.
The 'more' and the 'less'
Are the laws of nature ...
The 'flood' and the 'drought'
Are normal cycles ...
At times it is 'give' and
At times it is 'take,'
Such days of varying fortunes,
Such days ... good and not so good ...
Fall in the lot by turns,
Time is made to change hands
Among nations and peoples;

Bay of Fundy — dry
Photo credit:
Mahmood Mustafa

When the day arrives with its trade,
The night waits in queue
And when the night spreads its peace,
The day takes a break
But they are still connected,
They are still tied ...
Without the one the other is meaningless,
Without the other, 'this' has no existence ...
They survive on each other's 'rivalry'
Yet promoting one another ...

And so also life and death ...
Like the ebb and the flow ...
Are intertwined and connected
If one is near the other is not far away
One shows while the other hides
And waits in the wings for its turn!
Till the gift of life is in your grasp
Live it ... live it to the full,
And when the basin is about to be emptied
Ebb away without complain,
Ebb away with calm,
Ebb away and join
That shore-less Ocean
Of peace and immortality ...
Gracefully!

*Bay of Fundy — water
Photo credit:
Mahmood Mustafa*

Mahmood Mustafa

THE BREAK-UP

That vast cosmos
And this tiny speck ...
Disunited
From fellow specks,
Or 'One Whole'
Broken in many,
One of which
Chosen and put to test;

Could this be something new?
Something sensational
With far-reaching consequences?
Could this be
The breaking up
Of an atom?

THE DISTANCE IS SHORT

From here to there ...
From the cradle to the grave
The distance is short ...
A very short distance,
Before wisdom dawned
And knowledge took root
Dusk had fallen
And the night was on ...
A very dark night,

How peaceful is the sleep,
How restful and how sound
Would depend on the direction
The day led you, and you led the day;
The night could also be one of pain,
Stress and distress,
A night of questioning,
A night of guilt, a night of chastisement,
Again, depending on where the day took you
And you took the day;

But wait ...
Before dusk turns crimson
And then dark and slips into night,
Before the door is finally shut
There is still some scope,
There is still some hope
There is still a crack to slip through
True repentance, true atonement,
True remorse and true regret ...
On the other side there is mercy ...
Immeasurable, infinite mercy!

Mahmood Mustafa

THE IRRESISTIBLE

Aware, awake and alive ...
Eternally,
Present ubiquitously,
All hearing all the time,
All seeing at once,
Whom slumber seizes not,
Nor does fatigue ...

Comprehending, computing
Processing, resolving
All affairs ... both secret and overt;
Most erudite, most lucid;
Besides whom there is none;

The Sovereign, the Holy,
The fountain of Peace
And Perfection,
The Guardian of Faith,
The Preserver of Safety,
The Exalted in Might,
The Irresistible,
The Supreme ... the Glorious!
High above the attributed false partners;

The Creator, the Evolver,
The Bestower of Forms, of Colours;
Possessing the Most Beautiful Names!
All that is in the heavens and on earth
Declaring Praise and Glory,
The Exalted in Might,
The Wise!
The Irresistible!

The Bridge and The Bend

Can there be anyone similar,
Parallel, comparable,
Anytime, anywhere?
Even as a shadow,
A vague suggestion?
A far cry, a far cry!

And as a Friend ...
Always faithful, always there,
Always ready to assist, to support,
A Friend of those who believe,
Bringing them out
Of every kind of darkness ...
Into light!

Mahmood Mustafa

AND THE RIVER FLOWS ON

Cup after cup,
Tear after tear
The river flows on …
Unmeasured, limitless!

Like this Express on rails,
The train of thoughts
Is also on a journey …
Touching, pulling into
All memory stations of the past,
Stopping, boarding, resting,
Speeding, slowing, stalling but
Unflinchingly and adamantly
Chugging along,
Continuing the journey
Begun long ago …

More like one fleeing from the past
Than one trying to catch the future!

AFFRANTO*!

Couldn't bid adieu,
Couldn't say goodbye,
And then there was that parting ...
Forever ...
Not a word, not a look,
Never to cross paths ... again?
Affranto!

All those years of love,
Yearning and caring,
All blown away in one
Instant,
As though that hard-earned,
Toiled-filled, patient life savings,
Squandered,
Affranto! Affranto!

What went wrong and where?
Who was at fault?
So easy to blame, to put names,
To point fingers
But the reality is unexplainable ...
Two broken hearts,
Two shattered minds,
Much, much pain ...
And even more anguish ...
Affranto! Affranto! Affranto!

---

*Italian word meaning: Heartbroken

Mahmood Mustafa

ONCE BORN

Once born, when am I dead?
I may move, transfer or pass away,
Maybe from the seen to the unseen
But will still be there ... somewhere!

Once born, when am I dead?
This home ... to that ...
From temporary to permanent
From substance to spirit;

When immortality fashions
It leaves the stamp of infinity,
Longevity and permanency
The handiwork of the Master lives on;

Once born ... I will live on
The drop disappears as it merges
Into the ocean but is still there ...
The speck into the whole ...
Finding perpetuity!

THE OTHER SIDE

The Sun never rises
It is the Earth that dips,
The morning does not come
It is brought forward,
The noon hardly climbs
It is just a question of heights,
When does the evening ebb?
It is a sign of progress,
And the night never descends
It is just the other side of the light!

Mahmood Mustafa

AN EVENING OF CALM

As I stood on the Whitby pier,
Looking over the lake,
Out into the west
The sun was preparing to set
Through a crowd of clouds,
Painting the canvas in various shades and hues,
Now ochre, now pink, now crimson
And now deep red ...
Setting the clouds
The water and the pier ablaze ...

And the reflection in the east,
Converse to this hectic action,
Very placid, very calm, very still,
The colour too, a muted cherry
Of both sky and water;
Two majestic puffs of clouds
On the horizon,
Like mountains high,
Stood with heads covered as though in snow
Wearing a light pinkish robe
And I, caught between these two
Spectacular panoramas
Stood breathless and amazed ...
At times facing the action in the west
At times turning back and absorbing
The tranquility in the east ...
Both stunning and enchanting!

And what a journey for the earth ...
Between the rising and the setting,
In just a 12-hour voyage ...
Traversing thousands of miles,

The Bridge and The Bend

Leaving half the globe lit and exposed
And displaying a multitude of cities
In its course ...
Rotating and orbiting at a blistering pace
Yet hardly a ripple in the cup of soup,
And its generous platter serving
Magnificent silver sunrises
And glorious golden sunsets!

What an evening ...
What an unexpected blessing ...
An evening of peace, serenity and calm,
An evening of learning and wisdom!

Sunset at Whitby pier, Ontario
Photo credit: Mahmood Mustafa

Mahmood Mustafa

TAKE COURAGE!

The past summons
One more time
And one more time
The future looks unsure,
Uncertain, tentative;
'Coming events cast their shadows?'
Sometimes departed events too
Leave long,
Deep, unending shadows,
That linger on
Dampening spirits,
Darkening hours and
Bringing days of gloom.

But should that
Let a life cave in and
Surrender?
No, it should never;
Life should, in fact,
Collect itself,
Pick up the broken pieces
Stand up to all odds...
Muster courage and hit back;
The only way to survive and live:
Rise, fight and prevail!

THOSE HIDDEN FANGS

None is good and none is fair
But that stab is always brutal ...
Most painful and hurting,
'The unkindest cut of all' ...
Which is served from the back;
And that is the only way cowards work,
Weaklings, unsure of themselves,
Bereft of confidence and knowledge,
No character, no self-worth,
No scruples, no morals,
Ruthless, malicious, mired in lies,
Aiming for high ranks and high towers
But conscious of their shortcomings;

So the only quick way to glory:
Strike from the back, in hiding,
Pretend and swear by friendship,
Become the closest, the dearest
And when complete trust is won
Covertly attack to destroy,
To take over what in truth is stolen
And couldn't have been achieved
By honesty and hard work,
For none of that is part of their genes;

Such hypocrites are wisely
Referred to as 'usurpers' ...
The 'Brutus' of every age ...
But let us believe and have faith
In that age-old adage
The one granny used to preach?
"What goes around ... comes around"!
So let us wait and watch
For the reckoning is not far,
It will be colossal and complete
When it descends!

Mahmood Mustafa

TO HAVE LOVED AND LOST!

*'Tis better to have loved and lost
Than never to have loved at all.' ... Alfred, Lord Tennyson*

To have loved,
And to have loved in a singular way:
Decades of wanting,
Waiting and wishing
And then losing ...
What was thought to be 'forever'
But still continuing
To love and live each day in memory
And reminiscence!

To have loved,
And to have loved in an exceptional way:
With distance, time, and events,
All conspiring,
Forming one formidable force,
On the other side
On the opposite side,
To challenge love
On each, single, unsure step.

And to have loved,
And lost and then
Unbelievably, found love again ...
To rekindle passions,
Slumbering and almost cold,
Resurrecting and
Reconstructing a broken life
And celebrating and attaining the essence ...

The Bridge and The Bend

But then, yet again,
To have lost,
And this time, undeniably,
And ultimately ... forever ...
Was worth it ...
Was better than
Never to have loved at all*!

Mahmood Mustafa

COLOURS

Colours …
And that too seven?
Spread through …
Flowing in a stream
From the sky
Down to the earth;

The smoke,
Rising from the embers,
Takes on the hues of the arc
And changes shades
As it passes through them
Rhythmically …
One by one
Now green, now blue,
Here indigo, there violet;
As the colourful evening
Gradually ebbs into dusk
My eyes slowly
Give up the fight with slumber
And the mind surrenders
To fatigue and the weight of the day;

Then through the
Delicate mesh of recollections,
Tiptoe beautiful images
And like that multi-coloured semicircle,
Come to paint my dreams …
And somehow melt into
The seven notes of music …
Leaving my mind in a strange flux between
Colour and melody …
Which spread the vast

The Bridge and The Bend

Canvas of the mind
With plenty of ochre, gold,
Rhythm and notes
And ...
You!

Mahmood Mustafa

THE FALLS

From a river
To the mighty falls
To a river ... once again ...
The torrent gushes forth
Unstoppable,
With fury and force;
But never for a moment
Wild or unruly
Uncontrollable or erratic,
Always flowing with disciple,
Diligence and dedication;

The centuries, for centuries,
Have stood by, witnessed
And dispersed,
This extraordinary spectacle,
This amazing feat of nature ...
One of its kind ...
And we, the fortunate few mortals,
Have every reason
To be thankful,
To be simply proud
To have been counted
From among the billions,
In that small ...
That very small selected band,
To behold and attest
And be blessed with Grace!

Niagara ... you thunder, you roar,
You rumble, you boom
But at times
I have also heard you whisper,

As you rise and you fall ...
Unbeatable, unsurpassed,
Unmatched, unstoppable,
On your passage
Of wonder and awe!

Below: Niagara Falls
Photo credit: unsplash.com

Mahmood Mustafa

JIHAD*

I am a Believer
And I am at Jihad …
Are you a Believer?
Will you join my struggle?

I am a Believer
I am at jihad,
If you are a Believer join me …

I am at the greater jihad with
That destructive menace that is 'self,'
That lurking evil within,
Which keeps prompting me
To do deeds for which
I am secretly ashamed;

That same 'self' which prods me
To lie, to cheat, to deceive, to hate;
That same 'self' which nudges me
To envy, to backbite, to spread rumours
To eye another's portion
To harbour malice;

I am a Believer
And I am at jihad
 … A huge battle
Defying the rebel within
Trying to overcome that devil,
I am at jihad with 'myself';

I am at jihad,
Staying put in the face of adversity,
Fighting injustice,
Fighting for the downtrodden
Giving due to the deserving,

Protecting the weak;
If you are also at Jihad
What is your goal?
Who are you fighting?
Where is your jihad?
It cannot be in death belts,
It cannot be in the market place,
It cannot be against unaware pedestrians,
Certainly not the innocents in schools
Or merry party-goers,
Or devotees in worship ...

Come, my friend, join me,
Let's take the fight within,
Deep within
Into our hearts ... inside our minds,
And fight that menace
And cleanse and purify
That sea of hatred ...
Let us spare the innocent ...
For one innocent death
Is the demise of all humanity!

Let us fight,
Let the struggle intensify,
Let us defeat that evil within
Let us tame that rebel 'self,'
Let there be a jihad ...
A jihad for peace world over!

---

*Jihad: Let there be a jihad (fight) first against yourself, against your selfish motives, against your mean, malicious and destructive self instead of spreading destruction and hatred in the name of religion, dogmas, racism, sectarianism. Let us first correct ourselves. The instructions are also to first wage war against your selfish desires. Physically you can stand up in jihad but only in self-defence, to protect the truth, to safeguard what is right.

Mahmood Mustafa

THE DIVINE MANDATE

It only begins to abound
When You allow it to grow,
It only comes around
When You let it go,

It only blossoms and thrives
When You allow it to thrive
It only lives and survives
When You allow it to survive.

When permitted, it blooms
Fresh from the fertile soil,
But the misled mortal assumes
It is solely from his toil;

When granted, we seldom count
The many blessings from above;
When denied we groan and flout
The grace, the unconditional love;

You cause the day to slip into night,
You cause the night to pass into day
You bring from the dead the living to sight
And from the living You take the dead away;

Life grows only when You let it grow!
Honour is conferred only when You bestow!
It is all Yours ... You give, You take,
It is all Yours ... You make, You break!

BUT IF THE WHILE ...

*'But if the while I think on thee, dear friend,
All losses are restor'd and sorrows end' ... Shakespeare*

Your thoughts, your words, although
Now only shadows, echoes from the past,
Are precious props that support
And hold up a whole life ...
From a journey of the 'long ago'
Into the voyage of the unseen ...

If not all, many losses are restored,
If not all, many sorrows surely end,
When you, dear friend, come back
From that cherished past and
Make a presence, a niche, a dent
In this huge vacuum that is within ...

The world sees the outer,
The polished outer, the cosmetic
And 'made-up' outer, with layers
Of falsehood slopped on,
A necessity for survival and at times needed
To conduct the daily mundane ...

But the 'within' ... a huge empty canvas
Without any form, figure or colour,
A vast wasteland, sans all vegetation,
A deep, dried up basin, bereft of that elixir of life,
An empty house from where the principal
Occupant seems to have departed ...
Rudely!

And in spite of all this ...
If the while I think of you, dear friend,
Many losses are restor'd, many sorrows end!

Mahmood Mustafa

CHEAP TRADE-OFF

Deaf, dumb and blind,
Void of all wisdom,
Still trying to drum
Sense in nonsense ...
Friend – you are lost,
Inventing your own
Shams, out of folly,
To believe, practice
And preach.

You do nothing but
Fill your within
With fire that you swallow,
Concealing the truth,
What a miserable purchase
For what a dear price!

You, my friend, are the one
Who buys error
In place of guidance,
Torment in place of forgiveness,
Evil in place of goodness;

What boldness, what flair
You show for the fire!

A DIRGE TO NEWTOWN*

Twenty delicate buds
Crushed and trampled
When Newtown erupted in madness;
And the 'devil' danced
With hands awash in innocent blood,
When the world stood by helpless
And 'time' itself seemed, somehow,
To have gone out of focus!

And where does that blood flow?
And where does the trail lead?
Does it stop at 'sick' Adam's doorstep?
No, it flows much beyond, much further
To the corridors of power …
There are other hands, invisible hands,
Hands full and stained with blood …
To the promoters of guns
To the protectors of guns!

And the nerve of the propagators
To suggest more guns:
"The victim should have been armed
So she could have blown
The head off the assailant"
The remedy to violence …
More violence?
And the rest of the world …
Terrorists?

Newtown, your fragile buds were trodden,
By callous, arrogant traders …
Traders of death, traders in guns.

Mahmood Mustafa

Ban those guns!
Silence those propagators!
Rescue our kids!

....

The Sandy Hook Elementary School shooting occurred on December 14, 2012, in Newtown, Connecticut, United States, when 20-year-old Adam Lanza shot and killed 26 people, including 20 children between six and seven years old, and six adult staff members. Before driving to the school, he shot and killed his mother at their Newtown home. As first responders arrived at the school, Lanza committed suicide by shooting himself in the head. – Wikipedia

YOUR ABODE

Your abode ... beyond the stars
Your presence near ...
Nearer than the jugular vein ...
You are in the breathing
You are in the heartbeat
You are in the deep silence ...
Your abode beyond the stars!

Your company, I feel,
Your presence, I see,
Your fragrance, I smell,
Your colours, I wear,
Your aura, I sense,
One instant here, one instant there ...
Your abode beyond the stars!

How pristine is the dust
That holds my soul,
This soul that is part
Of that eternal verve
The eternal verve that is everlasting,
Ever fresh, ever living,
Ageless, timeless ...
Your abode beyond the stars,
Your home here with the humble!

ADVANCE REVIEW FOR THE BRIDGE AND THE BEND

....

"In this volume of poetry, Mahmood Mustafa looks deep within himself, over the wide expanse of his adopted land and across the seas, marveling at Divine creation, nature's bounty, and complicated relationships, revisiting fleeting moments that leave lasting impressions.

He moves between the past, present and eternal, drawing inspiration from his holy book, from a line or phrase from the old masters Tennyson, Shelley, Shakespeare and the Sufi, mystic, philosopher and poet Rumi, their words taking him down unexplored paths. And he rages at the mercenaries of the world, at those who put profit before innocent lives, at those who are heedless of relationships, or shallow friends who promise much but fail to live up to their words.

There is a sense of wonder, of gratitude. A park, a stream, the seaside, the mountains, the vast and diverse beauty of Canada – all reach deep inside, often drawing a parallel between what he sees and words of wisdom we may have heard but perhaps not absorbed. All through there is the dawning sense of comprehension that time and age bring that we, on this little speck in an immeasurable universe, are truly blessed. Go to the park or the seaside or the mountains – or even your deck, patio or a quiet nook at home. Find quiet moments within and outside, read the poems and reflect.
You will be rewarded with a sense of inner peace and, perhaps, a deeper understanding of yourself. Relax, read, reflect."

— Saleem Syed-Ali, Senior Copy Editor with the Tampa Bay Times, Florida.

ABOUT THE POET
MAHMOOD MUSTAFA

Having worked for over a decade as a successful journalist in India and Dubai, UAE, Mahmood Mustafa migrated to Canada with his family in 1993. After a brief stint of freelance journalism, he began work in the immigration and settlement sector. He continued in the field for over 25 years, helping hundreds of immigrants and refugees start a new life in their new country. Mahmood served the last 11 years of his career as a settlement services manager and retired in 2019.

Born and raised in India, Mahmood completed his education from the prestigious Osmania University in Hyderabad with a focus on English Literature. After completing his studies, Mahmood briefly moved to England before returning to India to pursue a career in journalism. Having worked for English newspapers in India, he eventually relocated to Dubai in the United Arab Emirates to work with Khaleej Times, a leading English-language newspaper in the Middle East.

He continued to be an avid reader of English, Urdu and Hindi literature. His extensive travel around the world has influenced the style and theme of his work. His poetry forms a literary canvas painted by the complex hues of his study of philosophy, mysticism, and history. Mahmood tries to give each subject a very personal and original touch. He published two collections of poems in India. The Bridge and the Bend (2019) and Crossroads and Beyond (2015) are his two works in Canada.

www.ingramcontent.com/pod-product-compliance
Lightning Source LLC
Chambersburg PA
CBHW052207090526
44583CB00017BA/2412